introduction

by the Very Reverend David Leaning
Provost of Southwell

Visitors come to Southwell from all over the world - and the people of Nottinghamshire, and the people of Southwell in particular, are proud of this wonderful Cathedral and Parish Church, dedicated to the glory of God in honour of the Blessed Virgin Mary.

This revised Guide provides an excellent introduction to our history and the wonderful skill and craftsmanship of those who, through successive generations, have cared for the fabric, and enriched and adorned it with many wonderful gifts. Every visitor will be captured by some aspect of its beauty and enthralled by its atmosphere.

a detail from the Minster's West window

1

I am conscious of the debt of gratitude we owe to the many people who, today, serve the Minster - Stewards, Chaplains, Vergers, Churchwardens, Bellringers, Servers, Sidesmen, Rector Chori, Assistant Organist, the men and boys of the Music Foundation, Administrator and Clerical staff, Shop staff, Embroiderers and Needleworkers - to name but a few, in addition to the Residentiary Canons, Vicar Choral and others who share with me in leading the work and mission of the Minster. Some are full-time or part-time employees, most others are volunteers who love this House of God and give their time freely and willingly, to ensure its work continues.

Vicar's Court and The Residence

Occasionally I am asked *"What is this place for? What do you do?"* A good answer is given by Henry Thorold a great friend of Southwell, in his introduction to 'Cathedrals, Abbeys and Priories of England and Wales' (published in 1986 by Collins):-

a service in the nave

"Day after day, the cathedral is fulfilling its function: the worship of Almighty God. This is what the cathedrals were built for. It was a deep irrepressible, irresistible, religious impulse that drove men to build these churches; here the worship of God was to be offered. The vision of Heaven, the near presence of angels and saints, demanded that for a time every day, mortal man should detach himself from the cares, the pleasures, of this life, and concentrate on Him. It was faith that built these churches, raised these vaults and towers, faith that moved the masons, carpenters and glaziers to cut the stones, carve the stalls, fill the windows with jewel-like glass - the faith which moves mountains. These buildings were designed to bring Heaven to men and men to Heaven."

2

a wedding in the quire

Now, as through the centuries, our primary task is to ensure that God is worshipped faithfully, with love and devotion, each day in Morning and Evening Prayer and the celebration of the Eucharist. Thousands come each year to great services in the Nave, because we are the Cathedral Church of the Diocese of Southwell - parishioners of all ages come week by week for worship and on the important family occasions - baptisms, weddings and funerals - for we are a Parish Church as well.

We hope that our visitors and pilgrims will find time to pause and absorb its atmosphere of prayer and devotion and use the cards placed in the many chapels to offer their prayers along with ours.

May all who come to this holy place, turn aside and glimpse the eternity that awaits them!

As part of the church's outreach, many thousands of children visit the Minster each year in a programme known as "Time Travelling"

"Life is not hurrying
on to a
receding future,

nor hankering
after an
imagined past.

It is turning aside,
like Moses,
to the miracle of
the lit bush

to a brightness
that seemed as
transitory as
youth once

but it is the eternity
that awaits you"

R.S. Thomas
poet

3

plan of the minster

the Chapter House

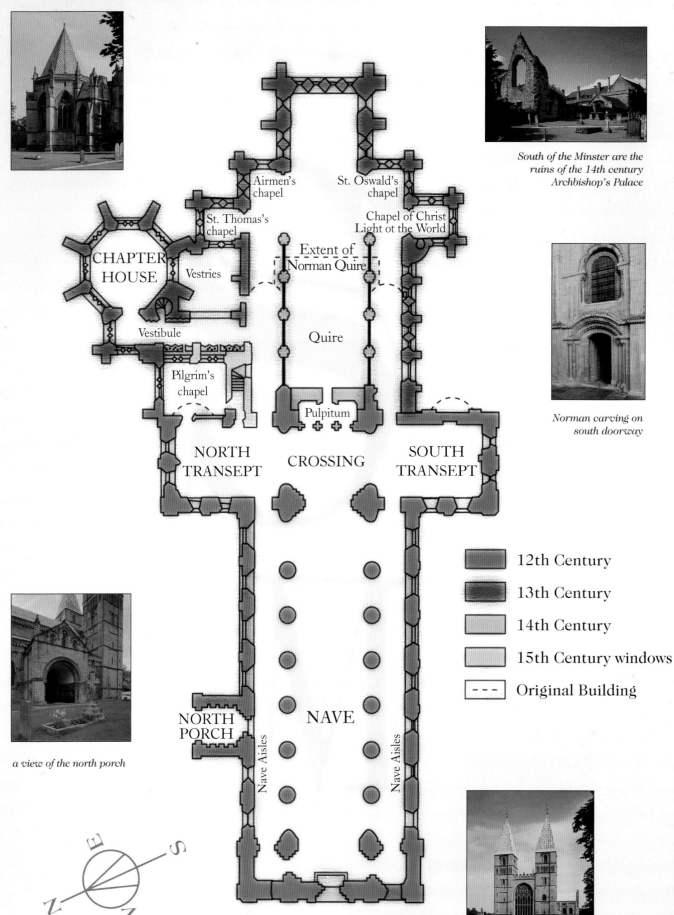

South of the Minster are the ruins of the 14th century Archbishop's Palace

Airmen's chapel

St. Oswald's chapel

St. Thomas's chapel

Chapel of Christ Light ot the World

CHAPTER HOUSE

Extent of Norman Quire

Vestries

Quire

Vestibule

Norman carving on south doorway

Pilgrim's chapel

Pulpitum

NORTH TRANSEPT

CROSSING

SOUTH TRANSEPT

4

NAVE

NORTH PORCH

Nave Aisles

Nave Aisles

a view of the north porch

■ 12th Century

■ 13th Century

□ 14th Century

□ 15th Century windows

--- Original Building

the distinctive 'pepper-pots' of the Minster's front

a tour of the minster

*Visitors normally enter by the NORTH PORCH.
If you have entered by one of the other doors
you should make your way to the north porch
where this descriptive tour begins.*

*the fascinating drip
mouldings depicting
Judas being swallowed
by Satan*

*the North
Porch of the
Minster*

5

THE NORTH PORCH is itself of great
interest. Stand outside on the grass and look at
the typical Norman windows above the entrance. Here can be seen on the
drip mouldings of the windows two '*Grotesques*', depicting Judas being
swallowed by Satan. Notice also the pierced right turret which betrays the
presence of a fireplace in the parvis room above the porch – the lodging of
the medieval Sacristan.

Inside the porch, the blind arcading on either
side leads to the magnificent doorway with its
seven orders of moulding including one with
'*beaks head*' decoration. The woodwork of
the door is 14th century. NOW ENTER THE
CHURCH.

*the blind arcading
of the porch*

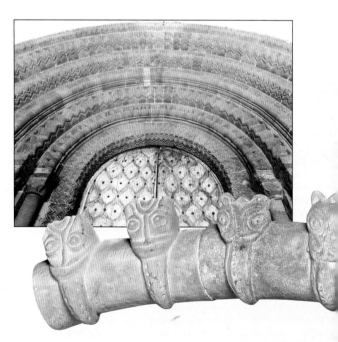

*Right; the porch
doorway with its
magnificent Norman
carvings with a detail
of the 'beaks heads'*

Let there be light!

6

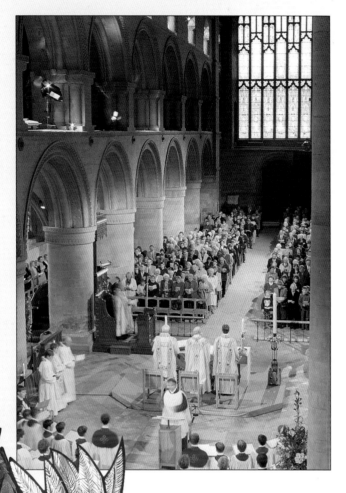

On entering, WALK TO THE CENTRE OF THE NAVE *and turn right, i.e. towards the west. Over the west door, the 15th century great* WEST WINDOW *faces you with its modern (1996) painted glass by Patrick Reyntiens blending so beautifully with the honey-coloured stone of this 12th century building.*

A television broadcast from the Nave

7

one of the pillars with decoration and the arches with their billet moulding

the font dating from 1661

Here you are at the heart of the nave and, looking around, you see an essentially Norman building, looking very much as it would have done to its builders. The squat circular pillars rise to broad triforium arches and above to the clerestory. There is little decoration except for the capitals and the billet moulding of the triforium arches. The wooden barrel vaulted roof is very much in keeping with the architecture of the nave but is, in fact, a 19th century replacement – the original roof being burnt out in a disastrous fire of 1711. To your left can be seen THE FONT which replaced the original which was destroyed during the Civil War. This font is one of several of the same pattern ordered as replacements by local churches on the restoration of the Monarchy in 1660. It is dated 1661.

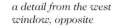

a detail from the west window, opposite

the nave-

*the Christus Rex above the crossing arch.
A great figure in wood, beaten copper and
gold leaf with outstretched arms,
welcoming, reigning*

8

Behind the font is A WINDOW OF *1851 by O'Connor where, below an illustration of our Lord's baptism in the Jordan, can be seen a reference to the traditional founder of the first church on this site c.630, namely St. Paulinus, wearing green vestments and bearing in his hand a model of the Minster.*

The wavy blue line denotes the river Trent. This end of the church has several windows by O'Connor, some of which were exhibited at the Great Exhibition of 1851.

stained glass window of 1851 by O'Connor and an enlargement (left) showing the founder of the first church at Southwell, St. Paulinus

9

Turning now to face the east, one is immediately aware of the powerful 'Christus Rex' BY PETER BALL (1987), hanging above the crossing arch. A great figure in wood, beaten copper and gold leaf with outstretched arms, welcoming, reigning.

Beneath is THE MODERN NAVE ALTAR AND CHOIR STALLS which give way on occasions to a concert platform erected for the many recitals, concerts and festivals for which the Minster is renowned.

Christus Rex

the nave lectern

To the right is THE PULPIT *by G.F. Bodley (1896) with carvings of the Virgin and Child, St.Augustine, St.Paulinus, King Edwin and Queen Ethelburga.*

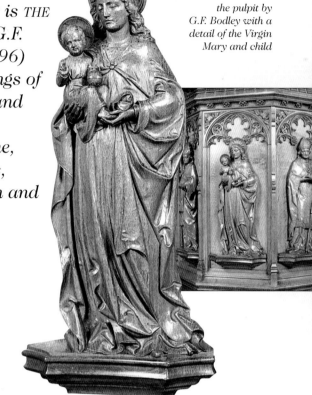

the pulpit by G.F. Bodley with a detail of the Virgin Mary and child

the nave organ

THE LECTERN, to the left, is a copy of the quire lectern. It has a fine wrought ironwork podium, with the words '*Laus Deo*' on the step. In this area can be seen the moveable console for the nave organ, which can be brought into the centre for recitals.

This fine modern instrument is housed above in the south triforium. A full specification of this and the quire organ can be obtained from the Minster shop, as can booklets on many other detailed aspects of the Minster's furnishings and architecture.

Move forward now into THE CROSSING. Facing you is the PULPITUM or QUIRE SCREEN (right). Built in c. 1340 in the Decorated style, the carvings are worth a study, particularly on the eastern side. Now turn right into the SOUTH TRANSEPT.

The earliest traces of the Saxon church can be seen underneath the so-called '*bread pews*' . This small paving is constructed from re-used Roman tesserae.

Above the pews is A MODERN CARVED PANEL '*The flight into Egypt*' by Robert Kiddey (1900-1984), a Nottinghamshire artist, above left.

On the opposite wall is THE WAR MEMORIAL BY CARÖE. Also on this wall is a *Pieta* carved by Peter Ball and some benefactions boards. By the south doorway A FINE COPE CHEST is situated.

wall plaster recovered from the cold bath house of a roman villa

11

Proceed now into the SOUTH QUIRE AISLE (left) passing on your left A MADONNA AND CHILD designed by Alan Colman for the S.S.M. chapel at Kelham and brought to the Minster on the closure of the chapel in 1952. To your right is A ROMAN PAINTING from the site of a bath house of a Roman villa close to the Minster and found during excavations in 1959, above right. Moving along the aisle the last window on the right contains FRAGMENTS OF MEDIEVAL GLASS put together in this window in l926.

a view of the vaulting of the south quire aisle

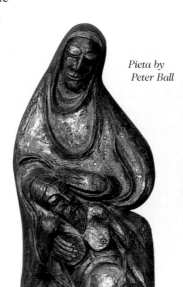

Pieta by Peter Ball

the Kelham Madonna

the chapel of Christ the light of the world

Now to your right is the first of THE ANCIENT CHANTRY CHAPELS,

the chapel of '*Christ the Light of the World*'. Here is yet another work by Peter Ball placed in the centre of the candle stand. This Chapel is used for private prayer and for petitions for those in distress (see notice board).

the Christ figure by Peter Ball dominates the chapel

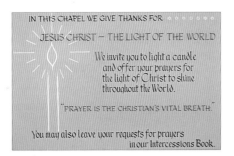

IN THIS CHAPEL WE GIVE THANKS FOR

JESUS CHRIST – THE LIGHT OF THE WORLD

We invite you to light a candle and offer your prayers for the light of Christ to shine throughout the World.

"PRAYER IS THE CHRISTIAN'S VITAL BREATH."

You may also leave your requests for prayers in our Intercessions Book.

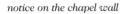

notice on the chapel wall

St. Oswald's Chapel

The next chapel contains A REREDOS BY CARÖE *and* A FRONTAL BY JOHN PIPER *depicting a raven, the symbol of St. Oswald.*

To the left is THE MEMORIAL TO BISHOP RIDDING, the first Bishop of Southwell. The figure, in bronze, is by F.W. Pomeroy and the base by Caröe.

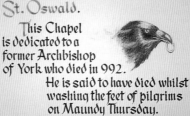

St. Oswald.

This Chapel is dedicated to a former Archbishop of York who died in 992.
He is said to have died whilst washing the feet of pilgrims on Maundy Thursday.

memorial to Bishop Ridding the first Bishop of Southwell

13

the sedilia dates from circa 1340

the high altar

the high altar

14

Move into the centre of
THE QUIRE *and stand facing
the high altar. Here is
craftsmanship in wood,
stone and glass, of different
ages but of high quality.*

a mouse in the Minster...

The altar rails and the furniture are from
the Robert Thompson workshop c. 1950
and are inscribed with his famous
'*mouse mark*'. THE UNUSUAL FIVE-SEATER
SEDILIA is contemporary with the
pulpitum (1340), although somewhat
restored in the early 19th century.

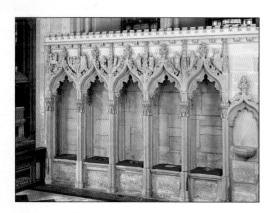

*the unusual
five-seater sedilia*

*mementos of the Royal
Maundy 1984*

*the lower four panes of the east window
are of 16th century Flemish glass*

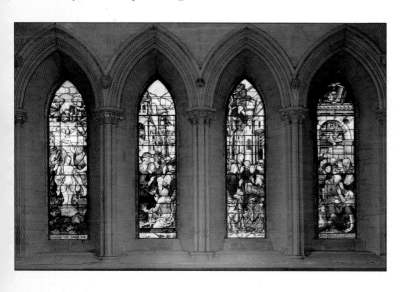

The glass of the upper
east window is by Clayton
and Bell (1876) but the lower four
panes are Flemish of the 16th century.
They were set in the Temple church in
Paris until the French Revolution but
bought by Galley Knight MP in 1818
and presented by him to the Minster.
Note the stone in the pavement
marking the visit of HM the Queen to
Southwell in 1984 for the Royal
Maundy ceremony. The quire pulpit is
another work by Caröe (1902).

the airmen's chapel

We next visit the two chapels to the north of the quire.
The first is known as THE AIRMEN'S CHAPEL *and contains*
RAF and Polish flags.

The altar was made in 1919 from the remains of aircraft of the 1914-18 war; the bench was made by RAF Newton in 1984 and the carpet with its RAF crest was presented by Elsie and Doris Waters. On the wall is A MEMORIAL TO THE MARTYRS OF KATYN designed by R.Sims (1987). THE REREDOS (1988) is a triptych by Hamish Moyle of the Little Gidding community and is based on a poem by Edith Sitwell - '*Still falls the rain*'. A MINIATURE TRIPTYCH on the table provides a full interpretation.

a memorial to the martyrs of Katyn by R. Sims

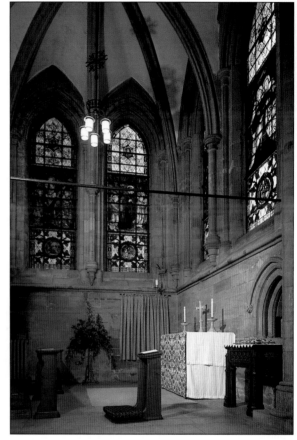

St. Thomas's chapel

St. Thomas's chapel

The next chapel to the north is that of St. Thomas.

This is the BLESSED SACRAMENT CHAPEL where the Sacrament is reserved for the sick and dying. The furnishings are by Thompson. This chapel is reserved for private prayer and you are requested to observe this usage.

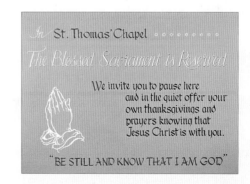

In St. Thomas' Chapel
The Blessed Sacrament is Reserved
We invite you to pause here and in the quiet offer your own thanksgivings and prayers knowing that Jesus Christ is with you.
"BE STILL AND KNOW THAT I AM GOD"

17

18

the quire

the quire

Return now to the centre of the quire and look around. The contrast with the style of the nave is apparent. Here clustered columns, rib vaulting and lancet windows display the lightness of the Early English style.

THE PULPITUM shows its more elaborate face and includes six return stalls with their 14TH CENTURY MISERICORDS.

Here also is A MAGNIFICENT 18TH CENTURY CANDELABRUM, and AN EARLY 16TH CENTURY BRASS LECTERN, found in a lake at Newstead Abbey in the 18th century.

The four blocks of stalls nearest the pulpitum (1886) are by Charles Simpson; the four easterly blocks by Caröe (1902).

Rising over the pulpitum is the 4-manual QUIRE ORGAN of 1996 by Nicholson which accompanies the daily worship of the Minster. It is housed in a splendid case, again by Caröe.

*the entrance to
the chapter house*

photograph Nick McCann

'the rich cornucopia of carvings is unsurpassed in accuracy, delicacy & variety'

the magnificent ribbed stone vault

the chapter house

Return to the NORTH QUIRE AISLE *where you will find the passageway entrance to* THE CHAPTER HOUSE.

photograph Nick McCann

The capitals of the 49 columns in the passageway and vestibule are covered in the foliage decoration to be found here and in the Chapter House itself and in both, the foliage is interrupted by portrait and caricature; note particularly as you enter, on your left, the carving of a demon on a man's head.

the entrance to the chapter house passage

Before entering the Chapter House pause in the vestibule and look at the exquisite carving of the doorway, surely the work of the Master Mason himself; vine leaves and grapes, buttercup, hawthorn, maple, potentilla, mulberry and oak all contribute to this exuberant display. This is the height of 13th century carving.

photograph Nick McCann

Now enter the Chapter House with its 36 seats for the Canons inscribed with the ancient titles referring to their livings. The capitals of the columns are finely carved in a variety of foliage. Hidden amongst the foliage, here and there, small animals have been introduced and in the canopies above some of the seats 'Green Men' can be identified. The tall windows with their small insertions of medieval glass lead the eye to the ribbed stone vault with carved bosses at the intersections. There is no central supporting pillar as one might expect, the weight being taken by the strong external buttresses.

carving featuring the head of a man - possibly one of the stonemasons

green man

Leave the Chapter House now and turn right to walk to THE NORTH TRANSEPT *passing on your right the entrance to* THE MINSTER LIBRARY.

In the transept to your right is a fine BRONZE OF SIR EDWYN HOSKYNS the 2nd Bishop of Southwell by Renolds Stevens and forward is THE MEMORIAL TOMB OF ARCHBISHOP SANDYS OF YORK who died in 1588. The Archbishop was one of four early Archbishops of York buried in the Minster - the tombs of the others having been destroyed.

memorial to Bishop Hoskyns (1904-1925)

Turn now to the west wall of the transept where over a doorway can be seen THE OLDEST STONE CARVING IN THE MINSTER, probably salvaged from the earlier church (date uncertain but possibly 11th century). St. Michael fights a dragon whose tail suggests Scandanavian influences. In the damaged left corner David rescues a lamb from a lion.

monument to Archbishop Edwyn Sandys who died in 1588

the saxon tympanum - the oldest carving in the minster

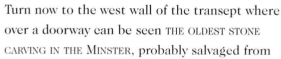

Turn round and descend a short flight of steps into THE PILGRIMS CHAPEL. This area originally contained two chapels situated side-by-side but was converted to the present chapel in the round and refurbished by R.Sims to commemorate the centenary of the Diocese in 1984. THE TAPESTRY, on the theme of pilgrimage, was presented by the Nottinghamshire Constabulary and made by Geraldine Brock (1990).

This completes this short tour of the Minster. We hope it has been enjoyable and interesting. The Pilgrims Chapel is a special place for visitors to the Minster and before you leave you may care to say a prayer for those you love and for those who work and worship in this place.

Further information about the Minster and its activities can be obtained from the information desk; from the Vergers and Stewards and from the Minster shop.

tapestry on the theme of pilgrimage, 1990 by Geraldine Brock

the story of Southwell Minster

The Cathedral and Parish Church of the Blessed Virgin Mary is popularly known, as it has been for centuries, as 'Southwell Minster'. From its origins, this was an independent church within the diocese of York, served by a group of priests, each of whom was supported by prebendal endowments of land and tithes dating back to Saxon times.

The group so formed was called a college and the church, which was the administrative centre of the area, was known as a *Minster*.

24

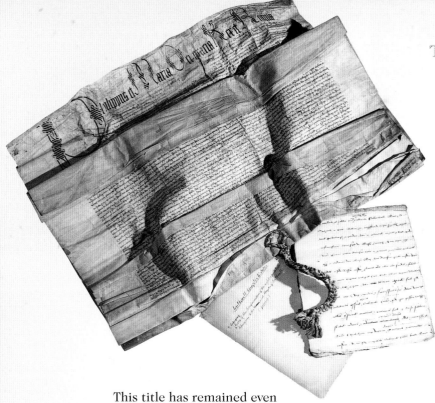

This title has remained even after the elevation of the church to Cathedral status in the 19th century. The See of York was a large one and its other collegiate foundations at Ripon and Beverley assisted in the administration of the western and eastern parts of the diocese respectively; Southwell being well sited to take care of the southern areas. The early Archbishops of York built and maintained a palace here until the middle of the 17th century, the ruins of which can still be seen to the south side of the church. Little is known for certain about the spread of Christianity in the post-Roman period but there is a strongly-held tradition that the first church on this site was founded by Paulinus early in the 7th century and an interesting window behind the font depicts, *inter alia*, Paulinus in Bishops' vestments holding in his hand a model of the Minster.

25

The earliest written record of the Minster is in a 14th century copy of a charter of c. 956 which records a grant of land at Southwell by King Eadwig (King of the English) to Oskytel, Archbishop of York, who established or re-formed the church with a body of clergy to serve it. By the early years of the 11th century the Minster held the relics of St. Eadburgh, daughter of a King of the East Angles, which would have made it a place of pilgrimage. A later Archbishop, Kinsius, gave two bells to Southwell c. 1050. His successor, Ealdred, founded prebends and built the first refectory where the prebendaries, or canons, might take their meals in common. So by the time of the Norman Conquest a collegiate foundation was fully established.

much of the Minster's history is contained within the precious 'white book'

Nothing of that early church remains except for the unique carved tympanum now positioned over the doorway in the north-west corner of the north transept; and some fragments of tessellated paving, probably taken from a 3rd century Roman villa nearby, which can be seen beneath the *'bread pews'* in the south transept.

*a south east view
of the Minster*

When Archbishop Thomas I
succeeded to the See of York in 1070, he found the church there
in ruins and the canons dispersed after the Norman Conquest. His first
priorities were the reconstruction of the church and chapter of York,
so it was not until the early part of the 12th century that his
successor Archbishop Thomas II was able to turn his attention to
Southwell.

As now, the church was some distance from the main centres of
population and possibly for that reason seems to have come
relatively unscathed through the Norman Conquest. At the
beginning of the 12th century, however, Archbishop Thomas II
in a letter addressed to all parishioners in Nottinghamshire,
begged them to assist in a new building at Southwell by
almsgiving. In return they would be released from their annual
visits to York and granted indulgencies. This letter, preserved in
the White Book of the Minster, established the Minster as the
Mother church of Nottinghamshire, and also identifies the start
of the work on this superb building c. 1108.

a stone carved head

As was usual, the construction started at the east and proceeded
westwards as money became available with the western towers being
completed approximately 50 years later. However, the original quire proved
to be too small and in the 13th century it was rebuilt to its present size.
The shape and size of the original are shown by the heavy dotted line on the
plan, from which it can be seen that the eastern termination was, unusually,
square and with apses – probably chapels – to the east of both
transepts. The quire aisles also terminated in apses. Traces
of the transept apses can still clearly be seen in the
east walls of the transepts.

The crossing, transepts, nave and western towers
remain substantially as completed in the 12th
century; one of the most perfect examples of
Romanesque architecture in England. The massive
quality of Norman building is seen here at its best. Note

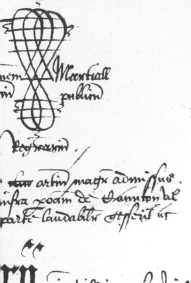

how the warm, cream-coloured Permian sandstone from Mansfield is laid with a smooth ashlared finish, and carved with bold ridge and roll, cable, and zigzag mouldings to decorate wall surfaces and arched openings. Such work compares favourably with the coarse tooling and lack of ornamentation of earlier Norman work elsewhere in the immediate post-Conquest years. The plain cylindrical piers of the nave arcade are squat in their proportion against the lofty crossing arches, but it is the repetition of wide openings in the triforium above which prevents the whole composition from being overbearing. The shallow capitals have differing formal designs in low relief. Each triforium arch has corbels at the springings and the stump of a shaft projecting down at the crown in preparation for an infilling. It would seem that an arrangement similar to that made, for example, at Romsey Abbey was intended, where subsidiary arches stand on a central column from which, in turn, a short shaft spans to the crown of the main arch. Such infilling was never completed by the Southwell masons. Higher up, at clerestory level, a passageway runs through the thickness of the wall; the windows externally being circular, a most unusual feature.

Seen from the churchyard the characteristic simplicity is even more apparent. Flat buttresses add very little strength but, together with the zigzag string courses, relieve and lighten the plain wall surfaces. The blind arcading on the upper stages of the North West tower is a design of intersecting arches; on the South West tower however, only the centre parts of the intersections are used, showing as lancet headed arches of the transitional period into Gothic. Almost certainly all three towers would have carried pyramidal spires originally, although perhaps lower than the present ones. The large traceried windows of the nave aisles and the great seven-light west window were inserted to lighten the dim interior in the 15th century.

a stone carving of God the father

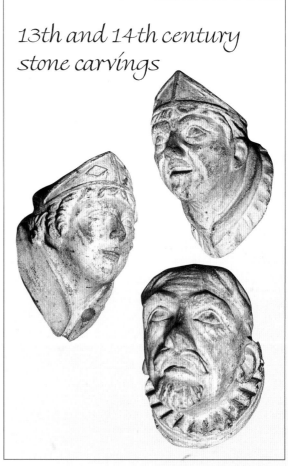

13th and 14th century stone carvings

Norman builders lavished fine workmanship on doorways and Southwell is no exception with the north porch being a particularly fine example. The entrance is barrel vaulted, and the walls decorated with a design of intersecting arches on short shafts. The first floor room, or parvis, is accessible only from the triforium and was probably for the Sacristan or his clerk who was required to sleep in the church and ring the bells at the appointed hours. The fireplace and chimney survive.

Apart from the geometric and formal mouldings mentioned above, decoration in the 12th century church is limited to the very few sculptured heads or grotesque masks on corbels supporting ribs to the aisle vaults in the nave, and the very interesting carvings in low relief on the eastward capitals of the crossing arches.

Although the office of Dean was created by Archbishop Thomas at York, Southwell continued in its pre-Conquest form having no designated Head of Chapter: the senior canon presiding at Chapter meetings and residence developing as a duty in rotation.

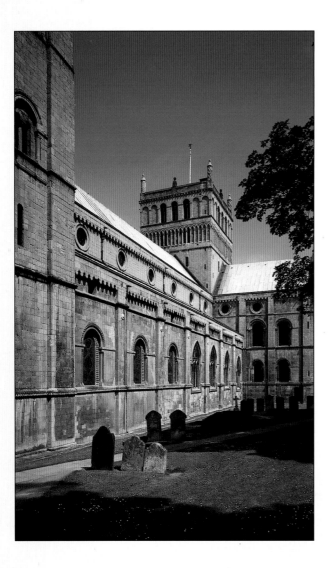

An event of some significance occurred in 1171 when a Bill of Pope Alexander III confirmed to the Chapter the privileges then exercised at Southwell by the Dean and Chapter of York. The Chapter became answerable, in theory at least, to no authority other than the Pope, although in practice the Archbishop of York remained the Official Visitor and exercised considerable influence. The number of prebendaries later became established at 16 and remained at this number until the dissolution of the College in the 19th century. Each prebendary was free to appoint his own vicar choral to maintain the Services and these also held amongst them the posts of Parish Vicar, Master of the Grammar School and other duties of the establishment. With 13 Chantry priests, deacons, choristers, clerks and others, the collegiate body grew to some 60 persons, of whom at least 47 were always in residence.

In 1233, Archbishop Walter De Grey issued letters of indulgence for those contributing to the work of the fabric at Southwell *'lately begun'*. This was to augment the resources of the Chapter in rebuilding the whole of the eastern end of the Minster beyond the crossing to accommodate the growing numbers of those serving the church.

the remains of the former Archbishop's Palace; the building was ravaged during the Civil War~ circa 1646

hatchment in the Minster of 1629 relating to Charles I

30

The Norman quire had been small in relation to the transepts and nave and this new project was still modest by comparison with the great cathedral at Lincoln, but the result is an exquisite example of the early English Gothic style. In the rebuilding, piers have been developed into clusters of keeled shafts terminating at their heads in plain but deeply undercut bell capitals; these support arches of vaulting ribs to the quadrapartite vaults which have matching grouped recessions of undercut mouldings, giving lightness to the whole structure.

The eastern end is squared, with shortened aisles, and chapels forming little eastern transepts. The triforium and clerestory are united behind twin lancet openings to simplify the composition. Some trace of the Norman piers of the crossing can still be seen although partially obscured by the later masonry. The stone of the quire carries a delicate blue veining contrasting with that of the nave.

Decorative carving in the quire is largely confined to the stiff-leaf decoration of the capitals and the dog-tooth moulding of the arches although a few heads are to be seen, amongst them the contemporary likenesses of Archbishop Walter De Grey and King Henry III.

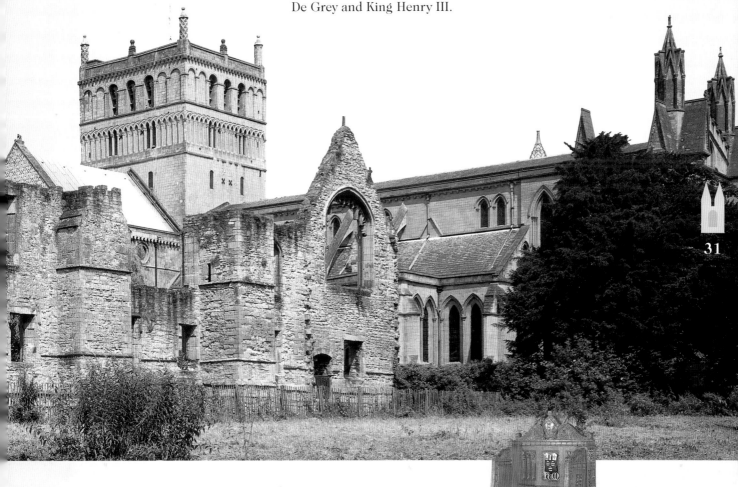

31

The eastern end was substantially completed by 1248, the last phase of the new building work being the construction circa 1260 of a chapel replacing the shallow apse in the east wall of the north transept. This is the present 'Pilgrims Chapel' ; the room above the vault now serving as the Library.

the Cathedra
(the Bishop's throne)

To the north of the quire lies the Chapter House, probably the most famous part of the building. The first reference to it is found in a decree of 1288 by Archbishop John le Romaine authorising the imposition of a levy on the prebendaries to assist in its construction. It would appear that the work had by then begun. In 1294 he also directed that fines imposed on the prebendaries as a result of their neglect of the prebendal houses be devoted to the fabric of the new Chapter House. The Chapter House is a regular octagon in plan, and linked back to the north aisle of the quire by a short passage and vestibule. To the east of the passageway stood a small courtyard in which the 'Holy Well' was located. This courtyard has subsequently been roofed over to form vestries.

Some modern glass by Patrick Reyntiens can be seen in the arches of the passageway. The design of the Chapter House marks another dramatic change in medieval architecture; the stone vaulting has no central pier to take the load which instead is carried on the massive stone buttresses at the angles.

The windows have slender mullions and contain delicate stone tracery instead of the limited forms of plain English lancets. The pattern of vaulting ribs also took a new and peculiarly English turn in design. The arched ribs which span diagonally from angle to opposite angle have additional, intermediate ribs between them which spring from the same piers but meet obliquely at the ridge instead of on the central boss. These are tiercerons - an English device in spite of the name. The junctions are developed with carved bosses which add to the richness of the effect. The outstanding achievement at Southwell was, however, the decorative stone carvings which spread over capitals and corbels, tympana, crockets and finials, vaulting shafts and bosses - a profusion of leaves, fruit and flowers from fields, hedgerows and forests, executed with a lively realism and a depth of perception never expressed before this time. 'The Leaves of Southwell' are world renowned. But there are also animals - goats, hares, birds and fabulous creatures – and human heads in portrait and caricature combining superstition and fable with religious beliefs. Altogether they are a vivid visual experience.

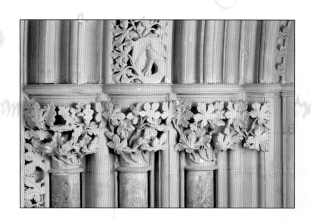

33

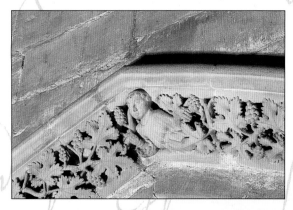

13th century carvings in the Chapter House

After the completion of the Chapter
House the next major work was the
construction of the pulpitum closing off the
west end of the quire. It provides a spectacular illustration of work of the
Decorated period and dates from c.1340. Seen from the crossing, three
richly carved canopied arches lead into a vaulted vestibule and there are
delicately carved heads of men and beasts to adorn them. The narrow
central arch gives a superb view past the 'Newstead lectern' of 1503 towards
the high altar. The east side of the pulpitum is even more lavishly
decorated, there being upwards of 300 carved heads to be seen on cusps,
spandrels and corbels. The six return stalls on the east side are furnished
with 14th century misericords.

The collegiate foundation weathered the storms of the Reformation under
Henry VIII only to suffer dissolution in the reign of Edward VI. Mary
restored the property of the Chapter as far as she was able and this was
confirmed in a series of statutes of Elizabeth in 1585, but it was a charter
granted by James I which again secured collegiate status to the church
beyond any doubt.

During the Civil War of the 17th century much damage was done
by Scottish troops to the Minster, and the Archbishop's Palace was
reduced to a ruin. However on the restoration of the Monarchy in
1660 the Chapter was reformed and for some years there was great
activity repairing the damage and neglect suffered by the church
since the Reformation.

The 18th century also brought its troubles. On 5th November 1711,
the spire on the south-west tower was struck by lightning and set on
fire. The fire spread to the roof of the nave and the central tower and
bells, clock and organ were destroyed. Restoration was put in hand
and completed within 7 years although with an unsatisfactory
ceiling in the nave which covered part of the west window. The
ceiling was removed in the 19th century when the present barrel
vaulted roof was installed.

Dissolution of the collegiate foundation came finally in an Act of 1840; after that date new canons were not appointed and the old prebendal properties passed to the Ecclesiastical Commissioners as the occupants died. The Minster was reduced to the status of an ordinary parish church, but even before the reorganisation was complete, it had become obvious that larger changes were necessary in the organisation of the Anglican church as a whole. In 1884 a new Diocese covering both Nottinghamshire and Derbyshire came into being, and the Minster was raised to its present Cathedral status. A separate Diocese was created in Derbyshire in 1927.

Early in the 19th century it was recognised that much further work on the fabric was required and the proposed elevation to Cathedral status added impetus to the plans. The work was carried out under the supervision of the Ecclesiastical Commissioners by the distinguished architect Ewan Christian. The spires on the western towers had, in fact, been removed in 1801 when their stability was in doubt, but after strengthening the towers it was decided to restore the spires but with added height thus creating *'the pepper pots'* as they are affectionately known in Southwell. The spire of the central tower, burnt out in 1711, was not replaced but the nave and transepts were re-roofed as one sees them today.

The medieval stained glass windows had been largely destroyed during the Civil War, so most of the present Minster glass dates from the Victorian restoration and includes fine windows by Kempe and O'Connor; notable exceptions being the 16th century Flemish glass in the four lower panels of the east window which were originally in the Temple church in Paris and the magnificent modern work by Patrick Reyntiens in the west window and the Chapter House passage.

35

14TH CENTURY MISERICORDS

The church today shows not only the great achievements of the previous centuries but the adaptation of a great and historic building to the needs of the present age.

The maintenance and restoration of the building continues; new organs, nave choir stalls, the magnificent new west window, and modern artwork are all to be seen. Across the churchyard a visitor centre, shop and refectory cater for the ever-increasing number of visitors. All this makes

the Minster Refectory

the Minster Bookshop